FAMILY DAY, A DAY THAT AMERICA NEEDS AGAIN!

Colonel Mike Miller

*FAMILY DAY, A DAY THAT AMERICA
NEEDS AGAIN!*
by Colonel Mike Miller

Printed in the United States of America

ISBN 978-1-60266-498-2

www.xulonpress.com

ACKNOWLEDGMENTS

I first want to thank GOD for sending me the best helpmate in the world, my beloved wife, Melissa. Second, the two greatest gifts from GOD beside my salvation are my beloved children, Sarah and Jacob who make family day complete. I want to thank my mentor in ministry, Pastor Dewayne Sadler for believing in me as a young minister. My Dad and Mom for raising me and always showing me love from above, Pastors Bob and Margaret Rodgers at Evangel World Prayer Center, where I received the leading to write this book during a time of PRAYER. Bishop Ed Kenney who has been my Spiritual Daddy for over seven years, Pastor Ron Gibson, my Pastor who has truly walked the life of FAITH!

THE GREATEST ACKNOWLEDGMENT I COULD GIVE IS TO MY LORD AND SAVIOR JESUS CHRIST! THIS COLONEL SALUTES YOU AS THE FOREVER COMMANDER IN CHIEF!

SPECIAL THANK YOU

I want to thank Good Shepherd Young Adult directors Bill and Gina Miller for their support, James D. Whitehead, my Father-In-Law for his support and prayers, Joyce Whitehead, my Mother-In-Law who has always been there for my family. Melissa Miller, my Wife and Best Friend for all the time spent helping me make this book a reality.

SPECIAL MEMORIAL

I want to thank Lt. Colonel Doug Sheehan from the Shively Police Department who passed away on March 19, 2005 after a battle with cancer. He was a dear friend and the greatest Law Enforcement mentor that I ever had. Sir, our vision of writing a book has become a reality.

TABLE OF CONTENTS

INTRODUCTION
(THE FAMILY)

*T*he title of this book was given to me in a time of prayer. When I was praying softly before GOD, he spoke to my spirit and told me that I was to write a book and call it; "FAMILY DAY, A DAY THAT AMERICA NEEDS AGAIN!" In my 16 years of ministry, I have never written a book, but I knew that I heard GOD speak into my spirit that the time was now.*

I want the readers to understand that I'm just a simple person, who awakes every morning and goes to work to make an honest living for his family. Being a fulltime Police Officer and Ordained Minister I see first hand the goodness of the Lord and the evil in the world. I know GOD has laid the responsibility of writing this book into my hands so that I can give you some instructions on how you can stop the enemy from destroying the most precious gift a human can have on this earth, THAT IS YOUR FAMILY!

I know as you begin to read this book, you will start to say that Colonel Mike is reading my mail and how does he know me so well. I don't know you personally, but the precious HOLY SPIRIT DOES! GOD wants you to know that the best ministry that you can have is your family. There are times in this book that you will laugh, cry, rejoice and may say how can GOD use a simple man like Colonel Mike. I am not a very talented man, I JUST KNOW HOW TO OBEY THE VOICE OF GOD.

The number one success in ministry or life that you can have today is to OBEY! In the 11 years of ministry that Melissa and I have shared together, we have always OBEYED the voice of the HOLY SPIRIT. I tell people that JESUS CHRIST didn't want to go to the cross and die, but he went out of obedience to our HEAVENLY FATHER!

Sometimes I wonder why many people stay in positions within the churches or the business field, is it out of loyalty? Please don't misunderstand me, I believe in loyalty.

YOU MUST OBEY THE HOLY SPIRIT, DO NOT BE DRIVEN BY LOYALTY. It was not loyalty that drove JESUS TO THE CROSS, IT WAS OBEDIENCE. The reason I share this with you is because this is what it will take to keep your family together. GOD wants you to obey him when it comes to keeping the family together.

My dog Zack is one of the most loyal things I have, he never says anything to hurt me, he turns circles when I come home from work, but there are times that he won't obey me. The word OBEY has been abused in the church and business world.

Obey, in the dictionary states: To carry out instructions; to be guided or controlled; to follow instructions.

(DOES THIS NOT SOUND LIKE – WHAT JESUS DID?)

This is what I tell people when I have to arrest them because they choose not to obey the law; (" SIT DOWN, SIT BACK, & BUCKLE YOUR SEATBELT," WE ARE GOING FOR A RIDE!)

I truly believe that GOD will touch your heart as you begin to read the chapters of this book! GOD BLESS YOU AND MAY THIS BOOK CHANGE THE DESTINY OF YOUR FAMILY TO DRAW YOU CLOSER TO EACH OTHER AND TO GOD!

CHAPTER 1:

HONEY, YOU'RE TOO BUSY

I remember back in the year 1999 when the *RIVER CITY LOVE SQUAD, INC. was birthed as a new ministry in Metro Louisville. I knew that GOD had called Melissa and I to start this ministry to help reach the HOMELESS and NEEDY in our community. I was investing 25 hours a week without pay with this new vision that GOD had given us, working about 50 hours a week at the police department and over 12 hours a week at my part time job at a department store working in security. I was putting in 87 hours a week and enjoying every minute of life until my wife approached me one day and said, "HONEY, YOU'RE TOO BUSY!" I looked at her and said, "WHAT DO YOU MEAN THAT I'M TOO BUSY?" Everything that I'm doing I'm doing for this family I told her.*

Melissa stated to me that I was not spending enough time with her or the kids. My first reaction to her was that she didn't appreciate all the hard work that I was putting in for our family and she was just being selfish.

Days, weeks and some months went by after that conversation that we had about be being too busy. Sometimes as men, we think we have all the answers; if that were true, GOD would not have given us helpmates. GOD started dealing with me about being too busy and one day while I was in a time of Morning Prayer, I asked GOD, "WHAT I'M I DOING WRONG?"

GOD reminded me of our conversation a few months before, that I didn't pay much attention to at the time. I said to GOD, "what do you want me to do?" GOD SAID, "GO BACK TO YOUR WIFE AND TALK TO HER!" I SAID, "OH GOD, DO I HAVE TO?" Of course being an obedient man was not what I wanted to be at that time; however, I went back to talk with her.

While having the conversation with my wife, we came up with an idea of having one day a week just for our immediate family and we would call it "FAMILY DAY!" This would be a day for Melissa and I to spend with our children. Here are some of the rules that we laid down at first:

1. Daddy could not take any calls.

2. *We would not let any event take the place of our family day.*
3. *There would be no fighting on Family Day.*
4. *We will do things that the whole family can enjoy.*

These were some of the basic rules that we started with in 1999.

I didn't realize how hard it would be to keep them, especially the first one. I remember the first couple of weeks I was breaking some of the rules.

I had my cell phone with me and would receive calls. You talk about getting a look from my wife; my response would be, " what Honey, I have to take this call because it is very important." I would then begin to see the disappointment in Melissa's eyes; and after the FAMILY DAY was over, she would remind me of all the rules I broke.

I remember watching an interview with Dr. Billy Graham on Trinity Broadcasting Network. I believe it was Dr. Paul Crouch who asked the question, "is there any regrets that you have, Dr. Graham?" I was saying to my self before he answered that question, THERE IS NO WAY HE HAS ANY REGRETS. This man has preached the gospel for over 60 years around the world and has been a personal friend and minister to many of our Presidents. He has lead more people to JESUS CHRIST than any other minister in the history of time. His ministry has always been a ministry of honor and has never been discredited in anyway.

Then his answer came, He said these two things:
1. *I WISH THAT I HAD SPENT MORE TIME WITH MY FAMILY.*
2. *I WISH I HAD READ THE BIBLE MORE.*

I thought I was going to have to call 911 when I heard his answers.

I had never seen him so humbled as I did that night.

I sat there overwhelmed with his response. I knew that Melissa and I were doing the right thing in having our family day once a week. When Dr. Graham spoke these words; "I WISH THAT I WOULD HAVE SPENT MORE TIME WITH MY FAMILY!" I thought to myself that was the best wisdom that I have ever heard in all the years I have been in the ministry.

We had the great opportunity of working with him in 2001 at the Crusade in Louisville, Kentucky where the River City Love Squad brought three buses of HOMELESS and NEEDY people at Dr. Graham's request.

If one of the greatest preachers of all time would make a statement about the family like this; should we not take this wisdom and change our way of thinking so we do not have to hear the words, "HONEY, YOU'RE TOO BUSY!"

You might be saying, Colonel Mike, you just don't know how important of a person that I am or how busy I am running my company, pastoring my church, coaching the ball team, making business deals. All these statements sound good, but they are only excuses to avoid the responsibility that GOD has given you as a man or woman to take care of the family.

We have heard this statement preached for years, "IT MUST BE GOD, FAMILY, AND THEN THE CHURCH." I believe that most people are living their life in this order, "CAREER, PLEASURE, MAYBE CHURCH, MAYBE FAMILY AND JUST MAYBE GOD FITS IN TOO!"

We all should remember that JESUS was a family man himself. Many times in scripture we see JESUS leaving the crowds, the business of the ministry, the mission that he was sent to do, just to spend time with his Heavenly Father.

I believe the greatest problem today with the family is that DADDY and MOMMY are just too busy, their not spending enough time or quality time with their family.

We must remember that one of the most impor-tant things that GOD has given us besides his son is the gift of time. How are you spending most of your time? I would encourage you to take a piece of paper and a pen to write down for one week the times that you share with your family. It will prob-

ably bring some concern to how little time you are really spending with your family.

Many times, as a police officer, I make runs where kids are left at home with no supervision. This is a major problem that we have in America today because parents are just too busy to find time to spend with their children.

Have you ever had to pay your respects at a young persons funeral? One of the most common statements that you will hear from a parent is that they wish they could have more time with them. I remember back in 1984 when my only brother was killed in a car collision at the age of 19. At that time I was 16 and the only thing that I could think about were the memories I spent with my brother. I could not think of anything else during that week of his funeral. Life goes by too fast for us not to spend the proper time with our family.

Have you heard these words lately, "HONEY YOU'RE TOO BUSY?" If you have, now is the time to ask GOD to give you a plan on how you can spend more time with the greatest gift that GOD has given you besides his son, JESUS CHRIST! THAT IS YOUR FAMILY!

I hope this chapter has opened your eyes a little, on how you may be spending your time. I'm not trying to tell you how to run your home, I'm writing this book from reality.

As we go into chapter two, together we will turn on our spiritual radars and look at how some of today's technology has hurt the family more than it has helped.

CHAPTER 2:

FAMILY (VS.) TECHNOLOGY

*B*efore *I really get started with this chapter, I want to make something perfectly clear. I AM NOT AGAINST TECHNOLOGY! As I am writing this book, I'm sitting in a police cruiser with radar, camera system, audio system and a lap top computer that makes my job so much easier in fighting crime and taking criminals off the streets of America. I have a cell phone myself, that at times I would like to throw in the trash.*

When you start your family day, one of the toughest things you will have to fight is the need to answer the cell phone. I do understand that there are professions that require you to be on call in case of an emergency. Occasions may arise that may cause you to cut your family day short, but don't allow this to be an every week thing.

While serving as directors of the RIVER CITY LOVE SQUAD, we would ask the staff not to call on our family day, unless someone died or somebody gave a million dollars to the ministry. I wanted my staff to realize how important family day was to me and that general problems could wait until I got back to work.

We sometimes think as leaders in businesses and churches that our immediate attention is essential. This is fatal thinking for the family. I would instruct my staff that a leader is only as good as the people they surround themselves with.

Everywhere you look today, you see someone with a cell phone glued to his or her ear. I believe we have that problem today because we want to appear like we are important people. Ask yourself this question, " what is more important, a cell phone or your family?"

That question might have offended some; I hope that it didn't! Remember, the mission of this book is to put your family at the top of the list and not the bottom. I'm so amazed when I see families out together and the parents have their cell phones glued to their ears. I always wonder if that call could have waited until the next day. Most of the time, the answer to that question is yes. I'm not saying that you should not take your cell phone with you on your family day, we choose only to receive calls in emergency cases. Maybe you work in the cell phone business and are thinking to yourself; "Colonel

Mike is trying to put me out of business." I want you to understand that is not my goal. Remember what I said earlier in this chapter, I thank the Lord for our technology today, but it must not come before the family.

In the summer of 2004 while I was on my way to the courthouse, I lost my cell phone. You would have thought by my reactions that an earthquake had just happened. I felt naked without a cell phone. I rushed home to call the cell company. I had to have another phone immediately and I couldn't go one more minute without it. You would have thought I was having a withdrawal like a drug addict. I spoke with the sales associate and she advised me to wait a couple of days, just to see if someone would possibly turn it in. I told her how important of a person that I was and without a cell phone I could not function as a police officer or minister. I had the sales associate rush me a new phone. I got it the next day and I felt like I had just got a fix. Later on that day I got a call from the county court house. A fellow police officer had found my phone and turned it in. I thought to myself, WOW, two cell phones, I will really look like an important person. What I want you to see in this story is that even cell phones can become a GOD to you! I know that some of you might be saying there is no way that a cell phone can become a GOD to me. Turn it off for a week and then let me know how you did.

Remember the first commandment that GOD gave to Moses, "THOU SHALL HAVE NO OTHER GODS BEFORE ME." As a police officer, I see so many motor vehicle collisions because of cell phones; they have even put a box to check for cell phone use on our motor vehicle collision reports. I'm not crusading for a federal law to ban cell phone use from cars. I'm trying to show those who want to see and hear the truth that cell phone misuse can damage the greatest gift that GOD has given you, THAT IS YOUR FAMILY!

I have people ask me all the time about gun control. My response to them is; "a firearm is harmless." It only becomes dangerous when people misuse it or when a young person is able to get access to it.

I feel the same way about cell phones. They are totally harmless, however, if we never turn them off, they could become very deadly to your family. Communication is one of the best gifts that you can have in your family. When I was a Youth Pastor for Good Shepherd Church, I had a young man that came to Youth Services who was very talented in music and today he has become very successful in the rapping business.

This young man's dad would come into our Youth Service; he'd pull cash out of his pocket to buy all the teen's pizza. One day this man called me on the phone and asked if I wanted all his Christian material he had collected over the past forty years. Without even thinking, I said yes sir!

Later that week he brought the material to me. Two weeks later that same man stuck a gun to his head called his son into his bedroom and shot himself. At that time I had been in Law Enforcement for five years and I should have seen some warning signs. However, because of the lack of communication I had with this man and thinking Christian people won't kill themselves, I just didn't think anything of it at the time. Since then I have wondered many times if I would have questioned him on why he was giving me his Christian material; just maybe he might be here today. I assisted my Senior Pastor with the funeral.

I shared this story with you to show how important communication is with your family. You may want to think about turning your cell phone off so you can talk to your family without being disturbed by some piece of plastic. Remember what my mission is in this book. I want you to make your family at the top of the list, not the bottom.

How many times have you been at church, movies, gradations or even a funeral service and a cell phone goes off? You probably think to yourself how rude can that be. Have you ever thought how your family feels when you go out to spend quality time together and you spend more time on the cell phone talking to people who your family might not even know. That is why I told you earlier we choose to answer only emergency calls on family day. It lets my family know that they're more important than any business I might have. Remember that cell phones have voice mail and you can get the message the next day. I have a question for you, how many times have you seen the President of the United States while he is addressing the people of America stop his speech to answer a call? NEVER, because he wants to make his speech personal to let you know how important that you are to him. I hope this chapter has given you some light about how cell phones can destroy one of the most important things that GOD has given you on this earth, which is your FAMILY. Remember, I'm not against cell phones; I use them on a regular basis, but I have learned to balance my time to let my family know that they mean more to me than something that rings and vibrates.

As we go into chapter 3, I start to give you some ideas that will help you to start spending that quality time that you need with your family every week, so turn those cell phones off so you won't be disturbed when you begin chapter 3!

CHAPTER 3:

ONLY ONE DAY A WEEK

*I*n this chapter I give you some steps on how to start your family day. I know that we all live busy lives, but in order for your family to stay together you must develop a plan, a schedule and stick to them both. As for my family, our family day's change due to my rotating schedule. I always write family days on my calendar so my wife and children will know when family day will be.*

I'm going to give you three steps on how to start this:

<u>STEP 1</u>
You must sit down with your family to pick a day that you can spend together as a family. Remember GOD IS PRO-FAMILY. As I said in chapter 2, there are some professions that might require you to be called out while you are spending time with your family. If that happens, you need to make up

the time before the week ends. Make your family day a priority. I would start with a minimum of 4 hours together on family day. When you start this, it will be harder than you think to adjust your weekly schedules. For example, when you begin an exercise program and your body is not use to the work out, you may be aching the first few days but you know the results are worth the effort.

Working out for your family will bring results that will change the destiny of your home and children. I receive calls from fellow police officers and ministers wanting me to do things on my family day and I have to tell them that I can't because today is FAMILY DAY! I always get this response back, "WHAT IS FAMILY DAY?" I answer, "I'M SO GLAD THAT YOU ASKED!" Here is a couple of the responses that I get back after I explain to them what family day is:

    a. That's great, I wish I could do that, but my schedule is just too busy!

    b. Is there anyway you can do that another day!

The list goes on. There will be excuse after excuse not to designate a day with your family. Here's an example, a Pastor announces there will be a time of prayer at the church, he may only have 100 people show up out of a 1000 members. He will hear a dozen excuses, why the missing members couldn't attend. Everyone is just too busy to pray. However the same Pastor announces there will be a dinner at the church, you'll see 1500 people show up then! Why is that? It takes discipline to pray, there is not much discipline in eating. I promise you, it will take discipline to not allow the excuses to over take your family day!

STEP 2

You must do something the entire family will enjoy. I know that we all have different likes and dislikes, but I will give you some ideas that have worked for us. Each week we take turns on deciding what restaurant we will eat at and what type of activity that we are going to do that day. For example, here are activities my family does together: bowling, movies (must be clean), family fun parks, walks in our neighborhood, board games at the house, prayer time, and there are many more that you may come up with on your own, the most important thing is that you are together and not separated.

STEP 3

You must make a commitment that you are not going to fuss and fight! I know that you are probably laughing at this one, but this will be the hardest step and the one that you will be tempted the most to do.

Melissa and I really have to watch our kids on this one because there is seven year's difference between our daughter and son. They like to do different things, however, we remind them the most important thing is that we are all together as a family. I have to be honest, Melissa and I have to watch our tongues too because we like to eat at different restaurants and we like to do different things, that's just how GOD made us!

When you start doing these three steps, you will start to notice a big change in your family. You must stick with it. Remember this is your family and nothing can compare with that time that you are spending with them. If you truly love something, you will invest your time and resources in it. Many of you might have stock in the stock market and do very well on your returns and that is great, but why do you invest in that stock, because you believe it is going to bring a good return. I'm not trying to compare the family to the stock market, but the same principle applies with your family. If you will invest time and resources, you will get a great return on your relationships. What is more important to you? I will let you answer that question! Remember what my mission is in this book, to make your family at the top of the list and not the bottom.

I remember hearing a Pastor preach not long ago on human feelings and emotions. He said there are times when he doesn't feel saved or even know if he is a preacher; but he knows in his heart he is saved and he knows that he is a preacher. My point is you shouldn't make decisions based on how you feel. Feelings change from one moment to another. Feelings and emotions can mislead you if you are not careful. I don't want anyone to misunderstand me, I'm not against having feelings or emotions because both are apart of human nature, but I believe you would be much better off if you use these two important values, OBEDIENCE AND COMMITMENT! You will need to make a commitment to make these family days work each week!

When you start your family day, there will be some opposition that will try to side track you. The first will come from the devil himself, the bible says in John 10:10; "THE THIEF COMES ONLY TO STEAL, KILL AND DESTROY!" I can tell you from 16 years of experience as a street cop, the great destruction that I have seen in the families. I will not go into detail about everything I have seen, but will share some of my life experiences, about what it's like being a Police Officer in America. I have always liked this statement, "A FAMILY THAT PRAYS TOGETHER, STAYS TOGETHER!" I also like what I say, "A FAMILY THAT PLAYS TOGETHER, STAYS TOGETHER!"

You will have opposition from people that you love and admire, but you must not let anything come between you and your family day. I remember one Sunday night I was watching a preacher on Trinity Broadcasting Network. He was telling a story about himself making a decision not to go to church on Sunday night. He had stayed home to spend time with his family and watch ball games on TV. I thought to myself, he might face some opposition over that, however he gained my respect by making a decision to stay home with his family no matter what the opposition was going to be. We are talking about a Pastor of one of the largest churches in America and still growing.

Pastor, I would like to salute you for putting your family first.

I hope after reading this chapter you are now ready to start looking at a day in the week that you can spend with your family and you have already got some ideas about some of the things that you and your family are going to do on this special day.

As we go into chapter four, I will share some of my life experiences on making police runs to American homes!

Are you ready for chapter four? Let's go code three on this one!

CHAPTER 4:

" SEEING IS BELIEVING - THE BREAKDOWN OF THE FAMILY"

I *want you to know that I'm not trying to make this chapter a Cop's show! Remember what my mission is, to make your family at the top of the list and not the bottom. If I can help families see what will happen if they don't spend time together, I believe we can save a lot of families from destruction.*

As a police officer, I have to see things that the average person will never see with the human eye. I have people ask me all the time, "HOW CAN YOU BE A PREACHER AND A COP?" My reply, is what Jesus said when he was at the Sermon on the Mount, (Matthew 5:9) "BLESSED ARE THE PEACEMAKERS, FOR THEY WILL BE CALLED SONS OF GOD."

The Kentucky State Laws definition for a police Officer is; "A SWORN PEACE MAKER." I believe all states have similar definitions for a Police Officer. I also believe that preachers should be peacemakers because JESUS was a peacemaker. I do believe in standing for what is right morally in this country and will tell you whether I'm in uniform or out of it. I will stand for everything from Genesis to Revelation.

I want to start off by telling you something I see frequently as a police officer making runs in our city that disturbs me. THE KIDS ARE RUNNING THE HOUSE! I hope that statement didn't scare you, but it is the truth. I remember not long ago I made a domestic run to a house where the teenager was out of control. When I got there, I saw a teenager screaming at her mother and calling her every thing but mother! With a sincere look, the mother looked at me and said, "Officer, I can't discipline her because I'll go to jail!" I looked right back at her and said, "I'm standing right here, if you want to discipline her, go to town."

I had to eventually arrest this teenager because she had struck her mother in the face with her fist. This was a sad day in America that didn't make the front page of the newspaper or the top story of the local news.

Police Officers are making these types of runs everyday in America and it has gotten out of control; this is why you must have a family day so you can gain the respect and control of your home. I told that young lady that I would have never talked to my dad or mom like that; if I did, I would now have false teeth. I do not believe in physical abuse and will arrest anyone in a minute that is an abuser, but I do believe in spanking the behind if that is what it takes to get the job done. I did a lot of bad things outside the home that dad and mom didn't know about when I was growing up; but when I walked in the back door, it was YES MAM AND NO SIR.

I have made several runs where children were left at home alone; these types of runs are very alarming to me, not just as a Police Officer but also as a parent! Many of us have seen movies where children are left at HOME ALONE. We've laughed and thought it was one of the cutest movies we've ever seen. I do not want to discredit any of these movies, the actors or producers; but I will say, in reality this is no laughing matter! It is a serious problem today in America. When I go into these homes and see small children who where left at home because the parents are at work or just don't care, it grieves my heart! This is my reason for titling this chapter, "SEEING IS BELIEVEING - THE BREAKDOWN OF THE FAMILY!"

I remember on September 11, 2001 there was a local minister who was riding with me on patrol; he was interested in becoming our Police Chaplain. That was not the best day to ride with any police officer in America. The country was in a panic because we were being attacked on American soil. I remember we started to get 911 calls at a very high rate. We had people lining up at the gas pumps pulling guns on each other because they thought gas prices would go to five dollars a gallon.

We also had to make more domestic runs. One run in particular I recall was a teenager that had struck her mother because she did not want to do what her mother had ask her to do. I had to give this young lady a free ride to jail. The local minister could not believe what he was seeing and after I dropped him off later in the day, we never saw or heard from him again. I would guess he had a change of heart due to what he had seen. He pastors a great church in our city.

Remember what I told you earlier in this chapter, that police officers see more with their eyes than the average person. I hope you are now realizing how important it is to get the family together once a week so you can find out what is going on in each other's lives. As your children get older they're more interested in what they want to do or what is going on in their friends lives. My point is that you need to get to know them, what better way than spending a family day with them.

I would highly recommend if possible for mom to stay home with the kids until they are in their late teens. Moms, please don't shout me down just keep reading. I believe in working mothers because my wife was a working mom for the first two years of our marriage and was a single parent before we married. I understand that single parents do have to work to provide for their children.

I remember back to August of 1996 when my wife came to me and told me that she had been praying about resigning from her position at a local finance company. She came to me to discuss this decision. At that time she was making more a year then I was in Law Enforcement. Following our discussion, I told her there was no way she could quit her job. Later I was sharing with a dear friend and brother in the Lord about what Melissa and I had discussed. I remember this brother asking me a question that I have never forgotten. He said to me, "DO YOU BELIEVE THAT GOD WANTS YOUR WIFE TO STAY HOME TO RAISE YOUR CHILDREN?"

At first that question made me a little angry and I said, "I'm sure he does but we can't afford it." Then he responded back to me and said, "You know, Pastor Mike, you preach about having faith and believing GOD, can you believe GOD will provide for you so your wife can stay home and raise your children." At that time, my face turned red with more anger, but deep down I knew he was telling the truth! The old saying is the truth hurts sometimes. Weeks had passed after that conversation when I was riding in my police cruiser and I heard GOD say to my spirit, "Mike, can you trust me to provide?" I said yes Lord, but how will we make it when we're losing over half of our income not including benefits. All I could hear that day in my spirit was to trust him!

I called Melissa at work and told her that she could give her two weeks notice, so she could come home to do the most important job in the world, BEING A FULL-TIME HOMEMAKER! She was so excited and I was thinking to myself, have you lost your mind or what? However I acted like I was excited too. Currently, we have no debt other than our mortgage. GOD has blessed us abundantly. GOD WANTS TO BLESS YOU, BUT YOU MUST OBEY HIM! Melissa and I give him all the glory and honor. We have not missed a tithe payment in all these years and we still are able to give many offerings to feed the homeless, the poor and help other ministries.

I believe the reason that GOD has blessed us is because he wanted to show us how much families mean to him, and he knew one day that I would be writing this book.

I don't expect every mother to go out and quit her job just because you are reading my book. However, I will say what the word of GOD says in Jeremiah 32:27, "I AM THE LORD, THE GOD OF ALL MANKIND. IS ANYTHING TOO HARD FOR ME?"

Mothers, have you been praying about staying home with your children? Is it a dream or desire of yours? I would say this to you, "if you will pray and let the Holy Spirit guide you and your husband or family, he will tell you when and how." He can make that happen for you and your family! You must be in unity about this decision as a husband and wife, if not, it will not work!

To the single mothers who are reading this book right now you might be saying, how in the world do you expect me to stay home with my children? I will tell you that I don't have all the answers; but I believe that GOD could give you a job working from the home where you are more available to be with your children.

I believe if anyone has a true desire to spend more time with his or her family, GOD will make a way! Just be patience and pray for GOD TO SHOW YOU WHAT TO DO, AND HE WILL!

Sometimes we counsel with people before we go to GOD and that can be very dangerous at times. I'm not against getting good GODLY counsel from a Pastor or a trusted friend. Melissa and I have counseled with several people in our years of ministry, from millionaires to poor people.

We have had people come to us and tell us " GOD TOLD ME TO DO THIS!" We just look at them and say, "If GOD TOLD YOU TO DO THIS THEN YOU DON'T NEED OUR WISDOM, GOD IS BIGGER THAN US!"

I have seen people quit jobs, leave their families and do all kinds of crazy things just because someone told them to! That can be very dangerous to your family and career. I don't believe that the HOLY SPIRIT has ever given a wrong answer to anyone who truly seeks direction from above.

I could go on with cop stories all day. I wanted you to hear a couple of real life situations where the American Family is breaking down. We must turn this around and guess where it starts? If you said, the family you guessed right!

I hope after reading four chapters you are excited about getting your family on the right track, the best is yet to come.

As we go into chapter 5 you will begin to see and learn how important it is that family day should never be disrupted by anyone or anything. Remember what my mission is in this book, to make your family at the top of the list and not the bottom.

As we say in Law Enforcement; "LET'S ROLL" ON TO CHAPTER 5!"

A MILLION DOLLARS OR DEATH

*W*hen GOD called Melissa and I to start the RIVER CITY LOVE SQUAD, we started with a few people and $40.00 dollars. My mentor and Pastor, was totally behind this vision that GOD had given to us.

I salute Pastor Dewayne Sadler and his wife today for believing in that vision. Melissa and I served as Youth Pastors at this church for six years, and increased the youth groups' average of five to over 70 when we resigned the position. Pastor Sadler saw the drive and leading that we had from the Holy Spirit. He knew that GOD was birthing this new ministry for Melissa and I to be the founders and directors for a season of time.

The ministry started out as a small vision from a church of 150 members and today the ministry has over 130 members from every denomination working together to reach the HOMELESS and NEEDY in metro Louisville. It also has 40 active churches of all backgrounds, coming together to feed the poor every Monday night at an outside camp meeting service. The ministry has been in just about every newspaper in Louisville and has been top story on every local news channel in Louisville many times. We had the great privilege to be invited to speak about the ministry on Trinity Broadcasting Network, which is the largest Christian TV network in the world. You are probably saying to yourself, what does this have to do with the family and the title of this chapter. I'm so glad you ask! When this ministry started out, I did not have to invest too much time as the director due to it only being a one night a week outreach, but as the ministry began to grow and become more visible in the public, we started getting phone calls from people wanting to support the ministry. I had to invest more time meeting with pastors of churches who wanted to join us. I remember getting a call from a local businessman who donated a large amount of money, which at that time the ministry was getting ready to go under due to monetary reasons. We then began to experience a rapid growth and that is when it started to become a problem in my home. I was spending little time with my family. The words honey, your too busy became true. I was too blind to see that I was slowly losing my family due to the lack of time I was spending with them. That's when Melissa and I had our discussion on how to rebuild our family. After we prayed, we felt that the Holy Sprit had given us the idea, "Family Day!"

Melissa and I agreed that on this day I would not conduct any ministry work unless there was a death or someone donated a million dollars. We wanted to emphasize that it needed to be of utmost importance to interrupt our family day! Our saying became humorous with our staff. They loved the idea, and appreciated the time that we wanted to spend together as a family. We had the same policy not only on family day, but also on vacation time.

I know that sometimes we just will not listen to our spouse or our children. This can be very fatal to your family. I want to give you the definition for the word fatal:

CAUSING DEATH; DEADLY; BRINGING RUIN OR DISASTER; DESTRUCTIVE; DECISIVELY IMPORTANT; FATEFUL; BROUGHT ABOUT FATE; DESTINED; INEVITABLE.

Have you notice in your local paper or on the TV news of families that are killing each other with violent acts? It grieves my heart to see this happening. We must begin to put our families at the top of the list and not at the bottom. The day that I most look forward to at the beginning of the week is not church day, but my family day and then church. I believe if we would make a commitment to our families, it would change the course for the

43

American Family. They would begin to grow and love each other more instead of living separate lives. You will hear people say, IF I JUST HAD A MILLION DOLLARS LIFE WOULD BE GREAT. If that is the case, why are there so many people in Hollywood unhappy? Why are their families falling apart? I don't want anyone to think that I'm picking on Hollywood families, it goes for every family; but it is the Hollywood families that the media reports on for the world to see how their families are living and what becomes of them.

There are many homes that I go into as a Police Officer and all the money in the world could not fix that home. When I look at little children with tears running down their faces because Daddy and Mommy are fighting and have hurt each other in their presence I, begin to say to myself, "LORD, AMERICA NEEDS FAMILY DAY'S AGAIN!" You might say, Colonel Mike there is no perfect home! I will be the first to tell you that my home is not perfect, but since we began our family day there is so much more unity and peace in our home. We started with a plan that GOD gave to us and we call it family day.

I hope when you are done reading this book you pray and ask GOD to give you a plan to spend more time with your family.
We all must understand that no matter how big our ministry, company or as an individual we

become, our family must stay at the top of the list and not the bottom.

I truly believe with all my heart no matter how busy a father or mother becomes with their career, they still love their family with all their heart, they just don't know how to balance their career with their family, and that is when it becomes a problem, just like it did with me.

We just can't use that four- letter word anymore that we're too busy to spend time with our families.

As we take note from Hollywood not even a million dollars or fame can come before your family! I like the scripture in Matthew 16:26, "WHAT GOOD WILL IT BE FOR A MAN IF HE GAINS THE WHOLE WORLD, AND YET FORFEITS HIS SOUL? OR WHAT CAN A MAN GIVE IN EXHANGE FOR HIS SOUL?" Replace the word soul with family. Do I have you thinking now? I'm not trying to bring any disrespect by replacing words in the bible. I am trying to emphasize the importance of family. Remember what my mission is in this book, to make your family at the top of the list and not the bottom.

As we go into chapter 6, I hope to open your eyes regarding battles that all families are facing today!

CHAPTER 6:

DINNER AT THE TABLE

I want to salute all the families that sit down at the table and have dinner together.

I remember growing up as a child I would sit down every day with my Dad, Mom and brother and we would have our family dinner.

Since my brother's death in 1984, some of the greatest memories that I have of my brother were when I was sitting across the table from him, we were laughing and talking with our parents about the affairs of the day. Those memories I will take to my grave one day. Those were the days before we had a restaurant on every corner of America. I believe this is why we have no communication anymore due to the lack of time we spend at our dinner tables. The families are just too busy. I want the restaurant owners to understand right up front that I'm not speaking against the restaurant businesses, my family usually goes out to eat twice a week. Here is a plan Melissa and I came up with *that seems to work for us; maybe it will be of some use to you as well. We have dinner at the table at our house two days a week and then we go out to a restaurant two days a week which gives us four days a week to sit down together to talk and have dinner as a family. You might be saying to yourself, Colonel Mike, we got you beat; we sit down every day of the week! I salute you. This chapter is for families that don't ever sit down at all and there are many families across America who never sits down to have dinner as a family.*

I remember as a child growing up, I would be outside with my brother and our friends playing ball and then you would hear a loud voice say, "DONALD LEE AND MICHAEL LEE, IT IS DINNER TIME!"

You talk about taking off and running to your home because it was something that you looked forward to. If you were a minute late, Mom would let you know quickly, "you had better not be late next time."

There are times as an Officer when I'm patrolling the city streets, passing by homes in the city that have their windows down and out of all the years I have been patrolling these streets I may have heard these words a couple of times; "IT'S DINNER TIME." These are the words that America needs to hear again just not on Holidays, but everyday. If these words would echo through out our city streets and country roads crime would decrease so much that we would have to lay off police officers! I went into the military when I was eighteen years old and while I was in basic training I recall one of the rules that they had in the mess hall was that you could not talk during meals. It had a big impact on me because I came from a family that sat down at the table every night and had dinner. It made me realize how important it was to be able to sit down with your family and have dinner to discuss the things that were on your hearts and minds. I have thought to myself, maybe this is why we have so many people going to counseling sessions today and kids popping pills like it is candy. The dinner table just might be the solution to some of your problems that you are having in the home.

When Melissa and I were searching for our house. We observed that the kitchens were just too small! The house that I grew up in, the kitchen was the largest room in the house.

I sometimes wonder if the men who built those homes were building from their hearts and not building plans!

I made a run about a year ago to a house in our city that is probably one of the craziest and saddest runs that I have ever made in my Law Enforcement career. I was dispatched to a house on a family dispute between a Father and Daughter fighting over food. When I got there, I couldn't believe what I was hearing from the Father who called the police. The father began to tell me what had happened between himself and his daughter at the dinner table. They were both eating a sandwich and chips when the daughter reached over onto her father's plate and took one of his chips. As I begin to investigate the chip run, I started to question the daughter and why she reached over onto her father's plate and stole a chip. She stated that she just felt like it and was too lazy to get up and go to the kitchen counter where the bag was laying.

As I stood there I couldn't believe what I was hearing. At a family kitchen table there should be peace and love. You are probably saying, Colonel Mike, I can't believe things like this are really happening with families. This is why GOD put the inspiration of this book in my spirit. We must start sitting down at the dinner table again and having that open communication that families need so much in America again.

When I was a teenager and out of school for the summer, a friend and I had a job. We helped a gentleman pull up his sod so he could plant a garden. That man paid us fifty dollars apiece. I thought I was the richest person in the world and couldn't wait for my dad to get home so I could tell him at the dinner table. Just maybe, if we could get that excited about meeting at the dinner table again, things could change in America's homes for the better!

I hope after reading this chapter you see if the American families begin to have dinner at the table again, it could change the destiny of this great nation. I know this will not correct all the problems that the families are facing in the home. I guarantee it will help some of the problems you are facing with communication. Remember communication is one of the best tools that a family can have; there is no better place to keep that line open then sitting at the dinner table with the best gift that GOD has given you, that is your FAMILY!

I want to give you the definition of dinner:

THE MAIN MEAL OF THE DAY; A FORMAL MEAL HONORING SOMEONE.

If an important person were coming for dinner, you would make an extra effort for every thing to be just right. Well that important person is YOU! MAKE SURE YOU SHOW UP AT THE DINNER TABLE BECAUSE YOUR FAMILY NEEDS TO SEE YOUR FACE!

Most of us remember our favorite family TV shows many years ago. I believe in every episode you'd see the families at the dinner table discussing the daily affairs. We need to return to those days where dinner with the family is a priority.

As we go into chapter 7, turn your spiritual radars on so you can detect those things I'll be throwing your way. How much do you really know about your family or about GOD?

CHAPTER 7:

"I KNOW GOD, BUT WHO IS MY WIFE AND CHILDREN"

*I*n this chapter, I want you to realize that there will be times that you may want to lay this book down because of the truth. The enemy of your soul does not want you to hear this. The bible says in John 8:32, "THEN YOU WILL KNOW THE TRUTH, AND THE TRUTH WILL SET YOU FREE!"

We live in a society today where people just won't slow down for one minute to listen to GOD speak to their spirit about the direction that he has for their lives. As an Officer Of The Law, there has been many times that I run radar looking for speeders. It's not hard to find them. Some people just won't obey the speed limit laws. When I pull them over I hear every excuse you could think of and why they were speeding. Here are some examples along with my replies. I thought you might find it humorous and maybe you have even used some of these yourself:

1. *Officer, I have to use the restroom really bad!*

(You should have stopped somewhere.)

2. *Officer, I was just going with the flow of traffic!*

(If they drove off the bridge, would you?)

3. *Officer, Are you sure that your radar is working?*

(I'm sure it's been calibrated)

4. *Officer, I'm a Christian and shouldn't get a ticket!*

(The bible says to obey the laws of the land.)

5. *Officer, I have never had a ticket in my whole life.*

(There is a first time for everything.)

6. *Officer, I'm running late for work or school.*

(You need to get up earlier.)

7. *Officer, I know the Mayor!*

(That's good, so do I!)

8. *Officer, could you please give me a warning today?)*

(No warnings today!)

9. *Officer, I'm rushing to the hospital to see a family member! (You will be no help to them if you have a wreck!)*

Here is the last one and the only one that really matters to an officer when you are pulled over:

10. *Officer, I know I'm guilty of speeding and I truly apologize for my actions!*

(I have let many people out of tickets for making this statement due to them not using an excuse for their actions!)

Should you use this line if you get pulled over, I will not promise that you won't receive a ticket, however, the truth is always better then excuses.

I believe that families are so full of excuses to why they don't spend time together. It grieves the heart of GOD! Here are some excuses; do you see any you've made to keep from spending time with your family?

1. *I have to meet that deadline at work!*
2. *The Pastor is really counting on me to do that job!*
3. *I have to be there tonight because they're counting on me!*
4. *I'm doing this job to better our family!*
5. *I have to meet a friend tonight!*
6. *I have to go to a ballgame tonight!*
7. *No one else can do that job!*

The list could go on and on, my point is that everyone needs to stop using excuses and begin to say, "NO MATTER WHAT IS GOING ON TODAY, TODAY IS FAMILY DAY AND EVERYTHING ELSE CAN WAIT!"

When Melissa and I were Youth Pastors at Good Shepherd Church, we were so busy with the youth group that we knew who GOD was, but we did not know each other. We were at the church every time the doors flew open and at that time we were both working fulltime jobs. We had Sunday morning church where I taught Sunday school and then Sunday night service, Wednesday night service, staff meetings on Monday's, and Friday night youth activity. By the end of the week, I would look over at my wife and say, "GOD, I KNOW YOU, BUT WHO IS THIS WOMAN BESIDE ME AND WHO ARE THOSE KIDS!" I don't want any Pastor or Minister to think that I'm speaking against attending church or fulfilling what GOD has called you to do in your local church. I believe in the local churches, but I will say; "I believe the family comes first," without the family, you will not have a church. It was not long ago that our local newspaper did a national survey on the decline on church growth. The numbers were very alarming to me as a minister. I believe that I have the answer and its called, FAMILY DAY, A DAY THAT AMERICA NEEDS AGAIN! I truly believe if we will start to apply the principles in this book we will see the American Church grow at a rapid pace and membership would triple in a matter of months. We hear all the time about revival coming; I'm a true believer and convinced that revival MUST START IN THE AMERICAN HOME!

I want to give you the definition for the word HOME:

THE PLACE WHERE ONE RESIDES; A PLACE OF ORIGIN; ONE'S BIRTH- PLACE OR RESIDENCE DURING THE FORMATIVE YEARS; A PLACE ONE HOLDS DEAR BECAUSE OF PERSONAL FEELINGS OR RELATIONSHIPS; A PLACE OF SECURITY AND COMFORT.

No matter how many times you go on vacation, it is always good to come back home. Why is that? The answer is found in the last sentence of that defi- nition that I just gave you, because it is A PLACE OF SECURITY AND COMFORT!

As an officer, I can't begin to tell you how many teenagers that I meet on the streets that have no desire to go home! The reality is that a place they once loved and grew up in they now hate and have no desire to be there any longer! We must begin as leaders of our homes to start making family day a priority. Put your family at the top of the list and not the bottom! Attending church is not considered a family day, neither is inviting all your family over for a cookout. A family day is when your imme- diate family designates a day to spend together. Keep the communication line open. I believe that one of the most horrible runs we make as Police officers is when someone commits suicide. Our job is to investigate scenes of all kinds. I have noticed on suicide runs or attempted suicide that there was a breakdown of communication within the family! Why? WE HAVE BECOME TOO BUSY AND WE

ARE NOT SPENDING ENOUGH TIME OR THE RIGHT KIND OF TIME WITH OUR FAMILY!

I know that some of my fellow ministers will probably get upset with me in this paragraph, but remember what scripture I gave you at the beginning of this chapter about the truth.

Have you ever wondered why so many preacher's kids turn out to be the most destructive kid on the block! One reason may be that the pastor has been so busy taking care of the church needs that he failed to make his own family a priority, taking them for granted! THIS IS THE WRONG ANSWER MY FELLOW PREACHER!

Just because you're a minister doesn't exempt you from having family day's with your immediate family and I'm not talking about the family of GOD!

Well there goes all my scheduled church engagements out the door, but that's okay as long as it helps save one home. My mission in this book is to help put your family at the top of your list and not the bottom!

Melissa and I have counseled married couples that have looked at us and said, "I DON'T KNOW THIS PERSON THAT I AM MARRIED TO ANYMORE". Many times this statement is made because they quit spending time together. The more time that I spend with Melissa and the children, the better I get to know them.

As the director of the RIVER CITY LOVE SQUAD, INC. I would always tell my staff, if you love something, you would invest all your time and resources into it. I don't know how many times that I have witnessed a parent pull twenty dollars out of their pocket and tell their children to go find something to do, just get out of my hair. You should have taken the twenty dollars and said, "Let's go get an ice cream and sit down to talk." That would mean so much to your child and it let's them know that you want to spend time with them. If handing out money was the answer to helping the families of America, then why do we have so many problems in the families today? The answer to that question is that money will not take care of your family problems, time will. I understand that we have to make money to provide for our families, however, we cannot love money more than we do our family. I Timothy 6:10 says, "FOR THE LOVE OF MONEY IS A ROOT OF ALL KINDS OF EVIL. SOME PEOPLE, EAGER FOR MONEY, HAVE WANDERED FROM THE FAITH AND PIERCED THEMSELVES WITH MANY GRIEFS." Just as an example, if you replace the word faith with family in this scripture, it will show you just how important the family really is!

I told you that this chapter was going to be a hard one to take, but remember I have learned by experience. I do not want you to have to walk the road that I have with my family! Please don't misunderstand me. I'm the happiest man on earth because of my family and we have never been closer than we are today. That's only because Melissa and I have listened and obeyed GOD. Are you going to obey GOD when it comes to your family? I sure hope so; I wouldn't want to have to respond to a 911 call due to your family falling apart. When people call the police to their home, they usually want us to solve their family problems in five minutes. We can't solve years of problems in a few minutes but you have to start somewhere, how about today. Let's put your family at the top of the list and not the bottom.

As we go into chapter 8, we will deal with some rules and respect that you must have in your home before your family day can be complete!

CHAPTERS 8:

"HOW ABOUT SOME RULES AND RESPECT"

I believe that chapter 8 will open your eyes to another serious problem that faces our families today, that is the lack of respect in the home.

I frequently say when I am preaching, "DO YOU STILL LOVE ME? I HOPE SO!

I know that I will probably step on some toes in this chapter, but the most important thing is that by now your family is moving from the bottom of the list and making it's way to the top. I would like to say that I am not an expert on how to raise kids, but Melissa and I have raised our children according to the instruction of the Holy Bible and being lead by the Holy Spirit. We are so thankful for our daughter Sarah and our son Jacob. Our kids are not perfect, but they do respect and follow the rules that we have put before them.

In order to make family day a success, you must have your kids right in the center of the decision- making process. Our children look forward to family day, they can't wait until in arrives each week!

We ask our children to do their chores and to make sure they read their bible every day. We like for them to have these things done before we start our family day or any other activity. Our children have never complained about reading the word of GOD, however, they do complain about homework. Melissa and I know what the word of GOD has done for our lives and we want to pass that onto our children.

I told you earlier in this chapter, that Melissa and I are not experts on how to raise children, we do not hold any degrees and would not tell anyone how to raise their children.

We do not let outside influences tell us how to raise our children. I believe you should be very cautious to whom you let influence you on how you are raising your children.

I make many runs to homes in our city where kids are out of control. Some kids are running the homes because the parents have allowed them to. We have a school in our city we call the "LAST CHANCE SCHOOL" where we are called to just about every week. This is the last chance that these students have before they are dismissed for good from the public school system in our county. I have never seen so much disrespect in my life. Students assault teachers just about every week, fights go on every week, and students run away from the school everyday! They call the police and want us to solve these family problems in five minutes, most of the time we have to take them to jail because they want to fight us. I ask you the question, where have we gone wrong in America? My friend, the answer lies within our homes! We have used so many excuses why kids act this way that it has grieved the heart of GOD! We say they have medical problems, so we give them pills to pop. We say they come from a single home, so it is okay for them to act that way! EXCUSES, EXCUSES, EXCUSES!

I believe you understand the point that I'm trying to make. We have to stop using excuses and begin to see where the real problem has originated from, the family. Parents, dropping your kids off at church, the shopping malls or a friend's house will not solve the family problems at home; we must begin to teach our kids whom to respect in this order:

1. *GOD*
2. *THEMSELVES*
3. *THE PARENT*
4. *THOSE IN AUTHORITY (TEACHERS, POLICE OFFICERS, ELDERS)*

This was how I was taught to respect people in authority and I have done so all my life; I don't want anyone to think that I have never been disre-

spectful. We have all been disrespectful sometime during our lives and if you haven't, if you live long enough, you will.

When Melissa and I were Youth Pastors years ago, the number one rule in our Youth Services was you had to respect each other, the Youth Pastor and his staff! I remember one teenager who would come to our Youth Services every Wednesday night. He came from a home where his father had died and he was being raised by his mother and grandparents. He would come into our youth services and cause disorder and I had to literally ask him to leave many times. He would keep returning because he knew that we loved him. He was apart of the Youth Group for years and then his mother moved to the other side of the town and years had went by since we had heard from him. One day our phone rang, he was twenty years old and had called to thank me for teaching him about respect and that GOD is a healer! He told me when he was eighteen years old he developed a serious case of leukemia. The doctors told him that he would probably die within six months! He began to tell me that he remembered the times that I would preach from the word of GOD about JESUS being a healer. When the doctors gave him the bad news, his memory went back five years ago to me and the youth services. As tears began to roll down my face while we were on the phone, I began to thank GOD for what he had done in his life.

When Melissa and I had our new home built, we were at a Home Supply Store looking for our appliances and ran into him. He is now in his late twenty's married and has his own family. This story is true and goes to show you even if you come from a single-family home, if you have the word of GOD in your heart, GOD WILL HELP YOU OVERCOME ANYTHING THAT THE DEVIL MEANS FOR BAD! If you will begin to teach respect along with the word of GOD in your home, it just might be the answer to meeting your family needs. .

Many of the teenagers that Melissa and I pastored still visit or call us today because of the LOVE AND RESPECT they felt in our Youth Services! I want to salute all those who work with children and teenagers in all our great churches or ministries across America! I believe this is where the church truly comes into play to teach the children or teenagers that may have no structure to their family or no family time at all in their home. GOD can use that child or teenager to be the one who turns that family around.

As we go into chapter 9 we will begin to read, if the American Family does not regroup, we will be like the Titanic that struck an iceberg and began to sink slowly to the ocean floor.
By now, you may be tired of hearing me repeat this, but you only have to hear it again two more times, REMEMBER MY MISSION IS, TO MAKE

YOUR FAMILY AT THE TOP OF THE LIST AND NOT THE BOTTOM!

CHAPTER 9:

"WITHOUT THE FAMILY, AMERICA IS THE TITANTIC"

*T*he family is the most important thing that we have on the earth today, without it society would cease. If that were not a true statement then GOD would not have created Grandpa Adam and Grandma Eve. GOD would have just created the earth and animals and left it the way it was, but it was GOD himself who created the family. So I will ask you this question, if GOD created the family, do you think that maybe he might be a little concerned on how the family is acting today? You better believe that he is and he will hold us account-able if we don't make some changes. I truly believe that we are in a crossroad for the American Family. We must begin to STAND UP AND FIGHT FOR THE FAMILY, NO MATTER WHAT THE COST IS! Our voice must be heard louder than it has ever *been heard or the American Family will sink like the titantic. I know some may be reading this book and saying, Colonel Mike, are you only talking about the Christian Family? The answer is no, I'm talking about every family in America. I want to make it clear in this chapter that I am a born again Christian who loves the LORD JESUS with all his heart! As you know by reading this book that I have been in Law Enforcement for sixteen years and I have never treated anyone different when it comes to the law. However, I do not believe homosexuals make up the family. GOD started the family with a man and woman, Adam and Eve. Read; "GENESIS 2:22 and GENESIS 4:1." He made us to multiply and replenish the earth. All though I do not believe that a homosexual couple makes up the family GOD intended, I know He loves them. Before all my critics start asking me questions about this, I want you to understand that Melissa and I love homosexuals and have feed hundreds of them. We have given them new shoes, clothing and are still doing that today through the RIVER CITY LOVE SQUAD, INC. (www.rclsm.org) Since the birth of that ministry in 1999, we have ministered not only to homosexuals, but drunkards, adulterers, prostitutes, thieves, rich and poor. I want to reach all lifestyles with the truth of GOD'S word! So before anyone begins to throw rocks at me or my book, for taking a stand for the family; you may want to step out onto the streets to feed, clothe and reach thousands of lives, which are living the lifestyles that I just mentioned.*

You hear about sin creeping into the church. What concerns me the most is it creeps into the family first, then into the church, now into our schools, businesses and government. Do you see the chain reaction? Do you remember the first place that the devil went on earth?

According to Genesis Chapter 3 he invaded the family first.

Have you ever noticed that people who take a stand for the family seem to be attacked by others? I have personally seen pastors, men and women of GOD who have taken a stand for the family, attacked. We say, we all have freedom of speech that's what makes this nation great, but I ask you this; "DO WE; WHEN IT COMES TO THE WORD OF GOD?" Our nation says; we now have to separate Church from State. It's time we return back to the values our forefathers founded this nation on! I don't want anyone to think that I am trying to make this a political book, however, I will tell you up front that I am a very conservative Democrat. I do not vote by party line, I vote with my heart! It seems like a lot of the media wants to attack those Men and Women who want to promote the family and they want to call them bigots!

Here's the meaning of the word bigot:

A PERSON WHO IS FANATICALLY DEVOTED TO ONE GROUP, RELIGION, POLITICS, OR RACE.

I will always stand for the Family and for the religious freedom that our forefathers came here to establish in this great nation that we call America! One problem we have today is people hating each other because of their skin color. Why is this? I believe it's the way they were taught in their homes as children. This grieves the heart of GOD!

Do you now see why I have titled this chapter, "WITHOUT THE FAMILY, AMERICA IS THE TITANTIC?" The American home is the Titanic, the sin is the iceberg and the water that has begun to come in will be the destruction, should America not change it's course. This is why we must begin to fight for the American Family like never before if we want to change the course for our children and grandchildren. I will be asking the President of the United States to make a National Day for the Family. This nation needs to recognize the importance of the family, not only in America, but also around the world!

I remember watching a movie about the "Titanic." There was a part in the movie when the ship begins to sink and a family was holding hands and quoting Psalms 23 because they could not get on any of the lifeboats, they knew they were going to die. That image is in my mind today for the American Family, if we don't go back to spending time with our families, we will have to hold hands and start quoting Psalms Chapter 23 for ourselves.

Our homes will begin to sink, due to the iceberg of sin, which has no mercy.

I truly believe that we can turn the American Family around, but it will take time. This situation did not happen overnight and it will not be corrected overnight.

We do not have to sit back any more and let our families fall apart. We need to learn to use the word NO! There will be times when you start your family day and you will just have to tell people no, I can't make that deadline today, I can't make that golf game, I can't be on the bowling team, I can't, I can't, I can't, it's not a bad word if it's going to allow you to spend more time with your family! When Melissa and I were directors of the RIVER CITY LOVE SQUAD, we had a married couple on our staff who would never tell us no, just because they respected us. I asked them if they would just tell us no if they were unable to do something that we had asked them to do. Now you must use wisdom, you can't go to work tomorrow after reading this book and tell your boss that you're taking time off to start your family day because Colonel Mike told you to. Your employer may then tell you to come see me for a job! What I hope you will see is that most of us are committed to so many things outside our regular job that we do not spend time together as a Family!

Do you remember when you were a kid outside playing and you would fall down and get a scratch on your body and you would run to mom or dad for help? They would take you into the home and clean the scratch with some medicine, then cover it up with a band-aid. You would stop crying and begin to put a smile back on your face! I believe that we have to start cleaning up all the scratches we have left on our family and begin to get that spiritual medicine to start cleaning up the wounds in our homes. As I was writing this book during the month of June, I could not believe how many articles that I saw in the paper about families who were killing each other!

I knew this book was right on target to help show us that our families are the most precious gift that GOD has given to mankind. If that is not a true statement then why is the devil working so hard to destroy the families? Remember, the devil once was part of the family of GOD, but because of his rebellion and trying to be the head, GOD KICKED HIM OUT OF THE FAMILY. That is why he is trying to destroy every family in America! I hope that you will be wise enough to realize this when it knocks on your door!

After reading this chapter, your family should have moved to number 2 on the list!

I hope that in this chapter you truly see how important this mission is that GOD has given to me.

REMEMBER, MY MISSION IS TO MAKE YOUR FAMILY AT THE TOP OF THE LIST AND NOT THE BOTTOM! Let's roll into the final chapter and restore our families today.

As we go into chapter 10, I will share with you that today is the day to restore your family! I will never believe it is too late to restore a family or a human soul! The only time it's to late would be when you are placed into a coffin and lowered into the ground, that's when it is finished!

"RESTORE YOUR FAMILY TODAY"

I *want to start this chapter off by asking you a question, if you had 24 hours left to live, what would you do with those 24 hours? I don't believe you would say, I have to go work on a business deal, play golf, cut the grass and the list could go on! I truly believe that most everyone would want to spend that time with his or her immediate family. GOD has placed in our hearts the love that we have for our family! As a police officer I have made several runs to homes where love ones have passed away. Never have I heard one of the family members tell me that the person was a good businessman or could make the best deals, play the best golf game, or that they never missed a day's work, the list goes on! Hopefully, you get the point I'm trying to make. These are some of the things that I hear from family members.*

1. *The person was truly a great father or mother!*
2. *The person always put the family first!*
3. *The person was the corner stone and foundation for the family!*
4. *We are going to miss them so much!*
5. *I wish we could have had more time together!*
6. *Life went by so quick!*
7. *What will I do without them!*
8. *I never thought this day would come!*
9. *Why did this happen to them?*
10. *I wish I could have them back!*

I truly believe that all you think about when you lose a loved one is the special memories that you've had with them. In November of 2004, I had just got out of roll call from the police station and I was called on a run with a fellow officer, a woman who was taking her car and ramming it into other cars on a business lot in our city. As we were driving to the scene our radio dispatcher put out the description of the vehicle, it was a black ford explorer driven by a white female with extensive damage to the vehicle. As we proceeded to the scene, I was the lead car, as we drove around the curve, the black explorer was in my lane coming straight at me, she was driving over 60 mph! I remember saying to the LORD, do I hit her head on and take the chance of killing us both or do I leave the road way and take the chance of killing myself! Within two seconds, I made the decision to leave the roadway and as I was heading toward a telephone poll I remember saying, "LORD, IF I DIE TODAY, LET MELISSA AND THE KIDS KNOW HOW MUCH THAT I LOVE THEM"! Then I went through a telephone poll doing 50 mph and struck a tree before I came to a stop! It was a miracle of GOD that I only received a small bruise to my arm. The other officer later apprehended the woman, who ran me off the road. She was having family problems and had been taking loads of pills. I was later awarded a National Award in Law Enforcement for surviving that wreck.

I shared this story with you because as I was going off the roadway, I didn't think about anything, except the LORD AND MY FAMILY! I was not thinking about how much money I could make, how great of a job I did as a police officer, minister, or how well of a person I thought I was. I could only see the faces of Melissa, Sarah and Jacob, those precious gifts that GOD had given me.

There is a saying that I really believe is true and it goes like this, "A PICTURE IS WORTH A THOUSAND WORDS"! I love to carry pictures of my family in my wallet, there's nothing that means more to me in my wallet than pictures of my wife and kids!

There were times when I would go to my Grandma Miller's house and see pictures setting around her house. It was always great to see the love that my grandmother had for her family. She would share them with people when they came into her home. Where are your family pictures? Do you carry any with you? Do you have them hanging around your house or set them on your desk at work? I sure hope so!

It will take time to restore your family, but you need to start today!

Pray and ask GOD to show you how you can begin to restore your family! Remember what I said in chapter 1 of this book, Melissa and I prayed and GOD gave us a plan to pull our family together and since 1999, we have not missed a family day yet. We have missed other engagements, but we refuse to miss our family day! As you start to do this you will begin to see a big change in your family and even attitudes that we all develop because we become too busy with the things of the world! I truly believe that GOD had Melissa and I to resign from being the directors of the RIVER CITY LOVE SQUAD, INC. (www.rclsm.org), so we could write and publish this book to help American Families. We left a growing ministry because we wanted to obey GOD! Will you obey GOD for your family? Don't let the things of this world choke out the wonderful gift that GOD has given you.

Melissa and I would like to salute those who took the time to read this book. We would like to hear your testimony, in how this book and listening to the voice of GOD has changed your family.

GOD BLESS YOUR FAMILY!

CONTACT INFORMATION:

If you would like Colonel Mike Miller to come and speak at your church or group, contact us at;

FAMILY DAY,
A DAY THAT AMERCIA NEEDS AGAIN"!
Colonel Mike & Melissa Miller
(502) 424-0330
EMAIL ADDRESS: RCLSCAR1@INSIGHTBB.COM

Printed in the United States
117511LV00001B/22-60/A

9 781602 664982